Shared Space

Shared Space

Faith Bills

Shared Space

Copyright © 2016 by Faith M. Bills

This is a work of fiction. Any resemblance to actual persons, living or dead, or actual events is purely coincidental.

ISBN-13: 978-0-692-72783-6

ISBN-10: 0-692-72783-3

All rights reserved.
No part of this book may be reproduced or transmitted in any form or by any means.

For Grace

May these words guide you when I too am lost.

Author's Note

I began this book resolute, seeing the phases of life in black and white. I've since found contrast in revision, change to perception. To me the waning phase had just meant what comes after being full; less of a whole, lacking. In truth, the loss of the essential is vital to rebirth. You lose sight of the moon because it's on its way to becoming new.

Waxing

☽

shared space

Hanging, Pressed

Like a dried flower you stay put, a preserved idea on my wall. Gone but still mine until the slightest touch sheds your petals, and you exist no more; to anyone, to me.

shared space

Naiveté

I'm shaken subtly,
    you'd never know.
    I'm carefully quiet,
    on tips of toes.

Backtracking youth,
    I dare not speak.
    If love be deaf,
    then I be meek.

shared space

Humor

I'd rather run from falling,
      a deep pit it could be.

I'd feel a painful gnawing
      if the girl in love was me.

shared space

Forfeit

Forsaken flowerbeds,
    bulbs to plant
    but none shall grow.

Regretting already,
    mistakes I'll make
    ahead and down the road.

shared space

Ploy

Deceiving with truth,
    I lie to trick you.
    Yet I call all my bluffs,
    the trap does enough.

Blessed, my ruse,
    cons that mean nothing.
    This mess that I am,
    and forever becoming.

shared space

..As You Retreat, I Reread

I write to feel you later,
    my love, worth dwelling on.

The feelings only grow greater,
    as I reread and you're far gone.

shared space

Reciprocate

Longing for a beautiful, intangible love.
    If abundance would suit you,
    I'm shy of enough.

If thrill be your need, I'm calm as the sea.
    I'll romanticize the way
    you overlook me.

shared space

Endearment

Mistaken, sparingly so.
    An intimate addition
    to girls you fail to know.

I'll be off then in the meadows,
    plucking petals as you wish.

You'll be pressed between sheet and pillow,
    sealing her lips with a kiss.

shared space

Kismet

Unkind paranoia
    crawling up my spine.

What if he knows
    he's cherished so?

I want to make him mine.

shared space

All I Know

That your heart is beating,
    (for another).

That my heart is waiting,
    (for yours to discover).

shared space

Crescendo

Inattention keeps me at bay.
I wait for response,
suspending my days.

To shelve me
 will only stir up a swell.

I've said all,
 but not close to as much
 as I'd like to say.

shared space

Immutable

He hid behind his words,
    sealed his lips and seldom spoke.

He wrote to stay unheard,
    a weakness in his throat.

Extorting vocal stirs,
    I could be his antidote.

shared space

Beginnings

I'm sweet scents and summer rain, I come to relieve and change up your pace. I know what you need, I'd do most anything. I started to breathe when you first looked at me.

Small Steps

To see if love could last,
    a lunar landing held chance.

Would I be whole or hurt,
    once I went back to Earth?

Risk came with expedition,
    you were my Apollo mission.

shared space

Bygone

A canvas touched,
    a portrait begun.

An abandoned image,
    promised perfection but never finished.

shared space

Far Cries from Coherence

Hard feelings with a soft touch.

I longed to dive deep, mine to keep,
    though you weren't looking for much.

shared space

Immersion

Eyes glisten as you study something new,
    hopelessly dissecting each
    syllable I choose.

I pace my words,
    letting you win this
    lingual tug-a-war.

Though with time,
    eyes fell, pages turned
    and you grew bored.

shared space

Découvrir

A temporal sea,
    taken for what it was
    not what it is,
    or could be.

Drown in fantasies,
    love ashore-
    I wanted you,
    you wanted more.

shared space

Affection

Muddled deception on your tongue.

I heard a verse of love,
        but twas one of lust you sung.

shared space

Passade

Your lips, they did not promise.
    Your smile told no lies.

Your intentions, brazenly honest.
    The deception lay within your eyes.

shared space

Intent

I was blinded by another's hand,
    one I didn't hold.

Your words told promises you meant to keep,
    but instead had let fold.

shared space

Before You Leave

Don't kiss me,
      such promise would stain my lips.

Don't whisper,
      it's those sweet words I'd only miss.

Absence, Longing

A rose with no hue.
    A peak, lacking view.

Absence, longing,
    another day without you.

shared space

Repetition

Waiting unconsciously,
    even with my conscience clean,
    I tend to catch up with nonsense things.

Easing in cautiously,
    I bare to face another break,
    and shatter hope for sake of fate.

shared space

Run-on

I used to ridicule poets
    that romanticized 3am;
    but it's 4:40 and your dream
    woke me, and I now see
    the preciousness held
    between letting go
    my eyelids and
    giving into
    dreams...

        I'd still do anything for you,
        I'd still do anything.

shared space

Encore, Once More

"I've been here before- torn between knowing that you're nothing, and choosing to believe you're more."

shared space

Speed, Timing

If your light is ever present,
    your rays fixed, kiss my skin,
    love's still our disposition–
    could we begin again?

shared space

Reaching and Chasing

After all the aching,
    after my heart was split in two,
    after knees hit pavement
    and head touched ground for you.

I still think of only smiles,
    solely what went right,
    and yours is still the body
    I want to mirror mine at night.

shared space

From Sleeve To Chest

I know it's buried,
        that's how you hide it so well.

But it's there, I can show you,
        I promise not to kiss and tell.

shared space

Still Searching

Our souls left traces long before they belonged to us. Tracking markings on trees, footprints on the moon, I live a long-lasting scavenger hunt for you.

shared space

Distortion

Why do I still dream of chaos?
    All nightmares end with your return.

shared space

Chronology

I am a young girl and I sit in my treehouse, writing about all I hope for, a life shared, the songs I see in your eyes.

I am older and far less wise, still jotting with worn out ink and a weathered heart. I want much less, just a touch, a glimpse.
Je pense a toi, je pense a toi...

shared space

Carotid Robbery

He's done it,
    cunning culprit,
    once again he stole
    my heart.

Was above it,
    though I love it,
    when you break me
    entirely apart.

shared space

Exceptions

"I don't think I could make amends if it's pain I'll keep reliving."

"Then you do not know of love," she said, "it is forgiving."

shared space

Everything and All

Holding you,
   and feeling like
I'm regaining some life;
Jesus Christ.

shared space

Return

Recovered grins,
    tenderness, timelessness
as I'll drift endlessly, now
that you've let me back in.

shared space

The Roche Limit

A moon
> which wanders,
> will be torn.

A force
> is all,
> and none to blame.

A push
> was just
> the perfect touch.

To pull
> me back
> into your reign.

shared space

Ardor

I'd write a whole book
    to house just a sentence.

Give you one absent look,
    and pray ten days repentance.

shared space

You're Here, Once Again

The return of familiar,
        your scent in my sheets.

A surge of nostalgia,
        it's you that I breathe.

shared space

Sincerity

Gazing while others glance;

I can't live on the conditional,
I ache for things to last.

shared space

Totality

Long for no other,
it's all I will do.

Oust all unwanted attention,
for a little, from you.

shared space

Vierge

Skin untouched and ready.
    Your love, illustrious sin.

I've gotten over you,
    and only want back in.

shared space

Finir

Unexpected reversal,
    I had thought
    we'd been through.

Sudden switch
    from it's over,
    to it's always been you.

Full

○

shared space

Soliciting Fortune

There they were, two souls sharing the pasts and hopes of one another. Converging, even fate wondering what happened. They had destiny begging for what their future told.

Enamor

Partly consumed
    by the crescent moon,
    the meniscus that
    makes up your lips.

Perhaps tonight
    it's a sign in the stars
    that I wasn't
    supposed to miss.

shared space

Subdued

It's in the way I laugh.
    I feel it all, suddenly,
    and tilt my head back.

You retract, movements subtle,
    when irises match you
    you fumble with words.

For me the wounding
    is in your silence,
    the sweetest sound
    I've ever heard.

shared space

Certainty

His hands, the work of divinity.
    All he creates, so fine.
    Though love is all he's given me,
    how I wonder if he's truly mine.

I'm filled with all that I lack,
    his abstraction is perfect design.
    Grasping the small of my back,
    loved in this moment, that is all I can ask.

shared space

Sensory

Words can sink ships,
   I can read lips
   and I can feel temptation
   on your fingertips.

shared space

Fibs

I don't mean to tease, but much like tension it can't be helped.

shared space

June

Without doubt,
      without a question in mind.

We were certain,
      predetermined, and it was our time.

Fibonacci

An endless spiral,
    I delve absently,
        deeper and deeper into you.

shared space

Stars Formed

When you kiss me, I become broken glass. Your lips tempt love but bring only destruction. Each time, your mouth a weapon shattering me into different fragments, cracks with parting paths separating me from who I was.

When he kisses me, I feel a star form. A burst of nuclear energy creates us infinitely in that moment. I am no longer one but a unity, fused to greater skin. Immense atomic reaction separates who I am from who I've been.

shared space

Secrets

A swift embrace,
    chased with warmth
    and guarantee.

Exchanging touches,
    short-lived brushes,
    until it's only you and me.

shared space

Exodus

Surrounded by ferns,
    two hearts out of place
in a valley where no
life should grow.

shared space

Symmetry

Our brains they buzz together,
   a better love's nonesuch.
Who knew a whole divided
   could be worth so much.

Our minds they crave collective,
   our breath a currents kiss.
Hushed ache for affection,
   each other's touch well missed.

shared space

Salvation

In the form of your hands closing in on mine.

shared space

Illusions

Close encounters none have had
    with a light of your kind.

Though I've tried, I've failed to find
    what's in your rays that makes me blind.

shared space

Siren

A kiss
would only silence.
He prayed for
words to pour.

Abyss
she's trapped by shyness.
He'd drown in her
without leaving the shore.

shared space

Perpetual

Force that stands the test of time,
 our love outlasts both you & I.

shared space

Ceaseless

More than my waking thought- you've penetrated my dreams, past and present.

shared space

Us

You–

alight with life on your lips,
with light in your eyes,
with mine staring back
and a lost track of time.

shared space

On Portals

Engulfed were my hands,
   then my body
   fell through.
   Head first into space-
   seems my heart
   went on too.

shared space

Idyll

I love you with all
      omissions unused.

shared space

Choir

Sounds so sweet,
    enrapturing.

Your voice,
    our skin,
        the music we make.

shared space

Always, Forever

He's a story that holds me hostage,
    I'm trapped inside bound by spine.

I'm unable to break from this bondage,
    though I'd never see it fit to try.

Rêver

Streams of solitude
 as you whisper,
 leaves fall gently
 in the water.

Climbing trees to
 where I want to be;
 high up dreaming,
 in your canopy.

Divergence

He molds me to his liking,
      shapes my curves and lines.

Though no soul is similar,
      his craft's one of a kind.

shared space

Bane

The sky fell,
    my world stalled,
    when you'd tease me.

It was clear then
    that we could destroy
    each other so easily.

shared space

Stupor

I love a boy with deep brown eyes,
   his smile hides
   in sorrow's guise.

Weak of heart but sound in might,
   it must take a strong will
   to crush all of mine.

shared space

Awe

Can't process pictures of you
    without exposing light
    in the darkroom.

shared space

Change, Fluctuate

Your beauty deeply natural,
    body formed from lucent sky.

But your veneer goes down with sunset,
    bringing truth with the moon's rise.

shared space

Acts

Plagued by success,
    only concerned
    with being famed.

I was just an audition
    you showed up to, far too late.

shared space

Dolls

I've never played with dolls,
    though I've looked in your dead eyes.

You let me check an empty chest
    for hypothetical butterflies.

shared space

Rip Current

Holding on for life,
    hand in hand,
        I could've been saved.

You had it all,
    but lost me to the waves.

Misleading

Rosette, I bet
    she smells so sweet.

Heartless conquest—
    pricks all she meets.

shared space

Recherché

She walked towards me,
    and it became just two
    in a teeming room.

Surrounded by her light,
    she's made a thousand
    flowers bloom.

shared space

Je Veux…

Never had I formed a bond so swiftly,
    her words kissed me,
    she enclosed, enveloped
    like moss to a tree.

shared space

Appetite

Her eyes, my fated miasma.
    Trapped in her gaze I'm lost.

Her smile warns of disaster,
    as she greets me with desire's cost.

shared space

If They Ask

You think of the most lovely things that would never cross my mind.

shared space

Desire and Change

Voice like heaven,
  with eyes like hell.

She twists me
  to her liking,
    because she knows me well.

I'll never learn
  my lesson,
    this one thing proven true.

Manipulate my everything,
  I'd give it all for you.

shared space

Dusk

Chaste, my sun,
    stole my heart.
    Had me cursing
    when dark would come.

Yet unrequited,
    my advances stung.
    I couldn't wish her well,
    enough.

shared space

An Angel

Soft,
    and often unfelt by others–
    a petal never plucked,
    a stem left untouched,
    she longed for the hand
    of a lover.

Departing,
    far too soon–
    one had sealed her fate,
    on thorn he bled,
    farewell to breath, leaving her
    a faded red.

shared space

Another

I feel the loss the universe suffered as you conceived your last thought.

I consider you immortal; in my heart, still breathing.

Your grip is, as always, everlasting.

shared space

Eternal Love

Maybe instead, it is having an eternity in the brief time that you share. Compressing the endless, perpetuating what can't last forever.

Waning

☽

shared space

Suspend

As a child I'd often chase butterflies. A futile quest, trying to entrap something that was most beautiful when free. Still, I pursued them.

I find myself, now, caught up in the same enchantment that teased me in my youth. Unaccepting of impermanence, longing to freeze moments, as things tend to take off before I can hold them.

shared space

Lunacy

How do I take this tornado in both hands and compress it into words?

This time I'm not sure I can pave pain from just ordinary dirt.

shared space

Ghosts

I'm haunted,
    I'm followed
    by ghosts cherished so.

They're dead
    & they're gone,
    yet they still come and go.

shared space

Possessions

I warned him,
    he'd be wounded,
        though I was the casualty in the end.

He holds my heart
    so carelessly,
        and all I can grasp is this pen.

shared space

Subtleties

My hands on your chest, trying to permeate,
    let me in.

Your hands on my heart with loose grip,
    let me go.

shared space

Offerings

Our break a horror
    my heart couldn't face.

So my pen bled out,
    sacrificially, in my place.

shared space

Advantage, Pretense

Weakened with a racing heart
    I offered to replace-

Moving closer to your convenience,
    adding distance to our shared space.

shared space

False Convictions

Identical fingertips,
    I swore our love would fit.

Mismatched hands,
    we're out of place.

Still, something so sweet
    about pretending you were fate.

shared space

Terms

Nothing is precious. Lovers leave. Seasons change. Day inevitably becomes night.

We can hold onto sunsets; offer dusk all that we have, I hate to say it, but all beginnings beckon ends.

shared space

Anticipated Encounters

No remnants of you being,
      yet just before we stood so close.

And for this reason only,
      I am afraid I'm seeing ghosts.

shared space

Chronic Casualty

He is a mistake I'd make,
    again and again.

He is a habitual mistake-
    a pattern that must end.

shared space

Flee

We formed highways
    when our eyes gazed,
    our thoughts traveled all the time.

Yours commuted daily,
    falling victim to my fines.

The rising sun,
    a tollbooth tongue,
    to our demise
    love's made to run.

Stray

What have we become?
    Asteroids without purpose,
    orbiting a shared sun.

A hopeless galactic trip,
    passing time, losing life
    and celestial grip.

shared space

Undoing

Drainage of enamor,
      his smile's not the same.

The breakage that surrounds her,
      his bones, they'd formed a frame.

shared space

Parting Ways

You're moving away from me,
    what's there left to say?

As you loved conditionally,
    I fell into retrograde.

shared space

Forget Me, Not

Days without thought,
    I've faced just a few.

Forget-me-nots carried,
    I still think of you.

shared space

Stow Away

Though we're apart,
    I'm in memory, if you so choose.

Disguised in departure,
    do you walk around with me too?

Is It Deceit?

Contempt made light,
    seeing the passion in your spite,
    I'm pierced by a welcomed knife.

shared space

Arch Elements

I smile, reminiscent of those we used to share.

To you, I was extraordinary.
But against you, I didn't compare.

shared space

Thieves

Gardens grow in my mind,
    and he readily tends.

Cultivates only for harvest,
    conceding sincerity (now and then).

Of broken hearts I can avow,
    even pardon will not mend.

Bending for his will isn't worth it in the end.

shared space

Worth

Remarkably insignificant,
    only holding value
    when undressed.

His taste and touch
    meant nothing,
        and his word meant even less.

What Could Be

Love is a gamble,
> but you couldn't bear the cost.

What could've been our happiness
> now exists as your loss.

shared space

À La Vie, À La Mort

My happiness became yours,
    then severed, a fatal divide
    as you remain a corpse.

shared space

Games for Two

I would've stayed
    without pressure,
    without condition,
    I would've been your pawn.

It's taken a long time,
    but I'm starting to move on.

shared space

Smoke Signals

Won't you call me yours,
 slip my name into the void.

Now I'm all too sure,
 a mistake, naming love, a boy.

shared space

Then and Now

How we were
    when you played
    in warehouses,
    abandoned all habits,
    served as my cure.

How we are
    recurringly fleeting,
    love without meaning,
    a loss of all feeling
    I'd have preferred.

shared space

Decode

Deciphering messages on your lips,
    we kissed in code and often hid.

Unsure to mend or give,
    I seldom know if this is it.

shared space

He Was Mine

I loved him deeply
    though I held him briefly,
    his expression of passion
    came when he let me go.

shared space

Merged

They carry on as phantoms, silently haunting.
    I still face his ghost.

He turns away like I'm the stranger–
    though it's him I no longer know.

It's hard to believe it was his very hands
    I took as my own.

shared space

Skepticism

Curiosity held no candle to unsettled consent, it was compliance that killed me, indefinite intent.

Recall

I hoped you'd still be there, disrupting my orbit, a misplaced memory alive in my mind.

shared space

Pharos

Led me to safe landing,
       though our sense of security was false.

Your face, familiar structure
       of what was built to fall.

shared space

Ception

You absorb my light,
    then radiate it,
    but only to the blind.

Sticking to a feasible hoax
    so nobody catches the crime.

shared space

Truth

I know it means so little in honest retrospect, but your lips are still a pair I crave-

I miss kisses laced with threat.

Inverse

Love you only when you're leaving,
holding on to you
for all the wrong reasons.

shared space

Arousal

A second taste
    would more than do.
All I need,
    to fawn over you.

Of heart's awakening
    brought back an ache.
To have you again,
    surely my greatest mistake.

shared space

Lost Things

It's not a secret
    that I avoid the beneficial.
    Fillers only temporary,
    I replace damage with defect.

I'm moving slowly towards
    a life that welcomes dismissal.
    Reject me, break my heart,
    and I will be better yet.

shared space

The Rules

To want, without need.
        To long, without greed.
        To pursue, not acquire.
        To foster, not desire.

shared space

Au Revoir

"This day seems brighter than all others, and I claim no coincidence, but even I become radiant whenever you leave town."

shared space

Field Notes

You shouldn't love- but if you must, try to find someone with tender eyes, passionate hands, and apologetic lips.

shared space

For What It's Worth

It is both tremendously sad and beautiful to feel a distant love so deeply.

Though the planet is not conscious of the observer, the study holds no disparage.

shared space

What Survives

"I wish I could be present in my memories. Years relived, feelings again felt. I'll always be in love with the past."

shared space

Truest Love

I look back
>on our memories
>without anything breaking.

Though we're apart,
>you remain there—
>always waiting.

shared space

Useful Input

Do not expect.
    Do not overextend.
    Cast your sentiments elsewhere.
    Accept only love.

shared space

A First Mistake

Thinking you are anything less than angelic. You're not scarred from the mistakes made in your youth. No matter the wounds, your skin is still new.

shared space

Fader

We've gotten there; a point where the past feels so distant.

With time, you continue to drift from long gone, to non-existent.

shared space

Apologies

I'm sorry,
    I've let my heart travel.
    Sore from years of battle
    under siege from your attacks.

I don't know how it happened–
    I thought we were elastic,
    pulling to the point of breaking,
    but always snapping back.

shared space

Falling

Apart,
    in love
    and out,
    to pieces.

shared space

Sophistry

I feel for the love I once had,
        though it has made me only blue.

It is said that all good things go bad,
        antiquity pure in intent, it was true.

shared space

Significance

Daybreak to her was everything,
    til she beheld the beauty of nightfall.

Funny how something that holds all meaning
    can become nothing at all.

shared space

Disclaimer

Tell my love to pardon
 the pain I brought his chest.

It's better, blessed with ignorance,
 excuses are just reasons left undressed.

shared space

Metamorphosis

At attention, posture perfect
    hands decline the right to speak.

With shoulders back I dive right in,
    my words flooding even seas.

shared space

When Less Isn't More

What you deserve: a garden.

What you fall for: one rose.

shared space

Ebb

My reality became quite obsessive,
    fascination peaked & time moved slow.

Now I fall in love for just a second,
    but after that I let it go.

shared space

Inevitable

It was all temporal.

Our years were seconds until our days became compressed eternities.

Loving him, it was like seeing the far side of the moon. A mystery unveiled, a discovery I'd dreamed of- it meant everything for a moment.

But the wonder soon faded, and time began to transition, sand moved skyward and digits held no meaning.

It was all ephemeral, as hearts eventually stop beating.

Acknowledgments

To my sister, your existence is undoubtedly essential to my being.

To my mother, for showing me worth and strength.

To my father, for always reminding me to look at the moon.

To Claudia, I carry your crescent with me.

To the passing souls that come and go, I preserve of you all that I can.

To my dearest friends, I've yet to begin capturing the love you've shown me.

Index

Waxing

Absence, Longing... 45
Affection... 37
All I Know... 19
Ardor... 75
..As You Retreat, I Reread... 11
Before You Leave... 23
Beginnings... 25
Bygone... 29
Carotid Robbery... 65
Chronology... 63
Crescendo... 21
Découvrir... 35
Distortion... 61
Encore, Once More... 51
Endearment... 15
Everything and All... 69
Exceptions... 67
Far Cries from Coherence...31
Finir... 85
Forfeit... 7
From Sleeve to Chest... 57
Hanging, Pressed... 1
Humor... 5
Immersion... 33
Immutable... 23
Intent... 41
Kismet... 17
Naiveté... 3
Passade... 39
Ploy... 9
Reaching and Chasing... 55
Reciprocate... 13
Repetition... 47
Return... 71
Run-on... 49

Sincerity... 79
Small Steps... 27
Speed, Timing... 53
Still Searching... 59
The Roche Limit... 73
Totality... 81
Vierge... 83
You're Here, Once Again... 77

Full

Acts... 145
Always, Forever... 131
An Angel... 165
Another...167
Appetite... 157
Awe... 141
Bane... 137
Ceaseless... 121
Certainty... 95
Change, Fluctuate... 143
Choir...129
Desire and Change... 161
Divergence... 135
Dolls... 147
Dusk... 163
Enamor... 91
Eternal Love... 169
Exodus... 109
Fibonacci... 103
Fibs... 99
Idyll... 127
If They Ask... 159
Illusions... 115
Je Veux... 155
June... 101
Misleading... 151
On Portals... 125
Perpetual... 119
Recherché... 153
Rêver... 133

Rip Current... 149
Salvation... 113
Secrets... 107
Sensory... 97
Siren... 117
Soliciting Fortune... 89
Stars Formed... 105
Stupor... 139
Subdued... 93
Symmetry... 111
Us... 123

Waning

A First Mistake... 261
À La Vie, À La Mort... 217
Advantage, Pretense... 185
Anticipated Encounters... 191
Apologies... 265
Arch Elements... 209
Arousal... 243
Au Revoir... 249
Ception... 237
Chronic Casualty... 193
Decode... 225
Disclaimer... 273
Ebb... 279
Fader... 263
Falling... 267
False Convictions... 187
Field Notes... 251
Flee... 195
For What It's Worth... 253
Forget Me, Not... 203
Games for Two... 219
Ghosts... 177
He Was Mine... 227
Inevitable... 281
Inverse... 241
Is It Deceit?... 207
Lost Things... 245

Lunacy... 175
Merged... 229
Metamorphosis... 275
Offerings... 183
Parting Ways... 201
Pharos... 235
Possessions... 179
Recall... 233
Significance... 271
Skepticism... 231
Smoke Signals... 221
Sophistry... 269
Stray... 197
Stow Away... 205
Subtleties... 181
Suspend... 173
Terms... 189
The Rules... 247
Then and Now... 223
Thieves... 211
Truest Love... 257
Truth... 239
Undoing... 199
Useful Input... 259
What Could Be... 215
What Survives... 255
When Less Isn't More... 277
Worth... 213

www.ingramcontent.com/pod-product-compliance
Lightning Source LLC
Chambersburg PA
CBHW070138100426
42743CB00013B/2747